Yellow Umbrella Books are published by Capstone Press
151 Good Counsel Drive, P.O. Box 669, Mankato, Minnesota 56002
http://www.capstone-press.com

Library of Congress Cataloging-in-Publication Data
Jaffe, Elizabeth Dana.
    Can you eat a fraction?/by Elizabeth D. Jaffe.
    p. cm. — (Math)
    Includes index.
    Summary: Simple text and photographs introduce the concept of fractions and how they are written.
    ISBN 0-7368-1279-2
    1. Fractions—Juvenile literature. 2. Arithmetic. [1. Fractions.] I. Title. II. Series.
QA117 .J34 2002
513.26—dc21   2002016842

Editorial Credits
Susan Evento, Managing Editor/Product Develoment; Elizabeth Jaffe, Senior Editor; Jannike Hess, Designer; Kimberly Danger and Heidi Schoof, Photo Researchers
Photo Credits
Cover: Cathy Gyory; Title Page: Cathy Gyory; Page 2: Jean Higgins/Unicorn Stock (top), Dick Keen/Unicorn Stock (bottom); Page 3: Dennis Nolan/Picture Smith (top to bottom); Page 4: Index Stock; Page 5: Dennis Nolan/Picture Smith; Page 6: Cathy Gyory (top and bottom); Page 7: Cathy Gyory; Page 8: Photri-Microstock (top), Dennis Nolan/Picture Smith (bottom); Page 9: Carol Kitman; Page 10: Jim Shippee/Unicorn Stock (top), Kathy Adams Clark/KAC Productions (bottom), Page 11: David F. Clobes; Page 12: Cathy Gyory; Page 13: Dennis Nolan/Picture Smith (top), David F. Clobes (bottom); Page 14: David F. Clobes (top), Dennis Nolan/Picture Smith (bottom); Page 15: Dennis Nolan/Picture Smith (top left, top right), David F. Clobes (bottom); Page 16: Tom McCarthy/Unicorn Stock

Can You Eat a Fraction?

By Elizabeth D. Jaffe

Consulting Editor: Gail Saunders-Smith, Ph.D.
Consultants: Claudine Jellison and Patricia Williams,
Reading Recovery Teachers
Content Consultant: Johanna Kaufman,
Math Learning/Resource Director of the Dalton School

Yellow Umbrella Books

an imprint of Capstone Press
Mankato, Minnesota

The boy is eating **1** whole apple.

A whole apple can be cut
into equal parts.
Equal means
the same size.

These **3** whole apples are cut into **2**, **3**, and **4** equal parts.

1 whole apple  = **2** equal parts

1 whole apple  = **3** equal parts

1 whole apple  = **4** equal parts

Fractions are numbers that show how many equal parts there are of a whole.

This is **1** whole banana sundae.
This banana sundae is in **1** part.

She eats **1** part.

To write a fraction showing how many parts she eats, put the number of parts she eats on top. ⟶ $\dfrac{1}{1}$

Put the total number of parts on the bottom. ⟶

She eats $\dfrac{1}{1}$ of the banana sundae. She eats the whole sundae.

This is **1** whole sandwich.

This sandwich is cut into **2** equal parts.

She eats **1** part.

To write a fraction showing how many parts she eats, put the number of parts she eats on top. ⟶ $\dfrac{1}{2}$

Put the total number of parts on the bottom. ⟶

She eats $\dfrac{1}{2}$ of the sandwich.

This is **1** whole bowl of candy.

We divide the bowl of candy into **3** equal parts.

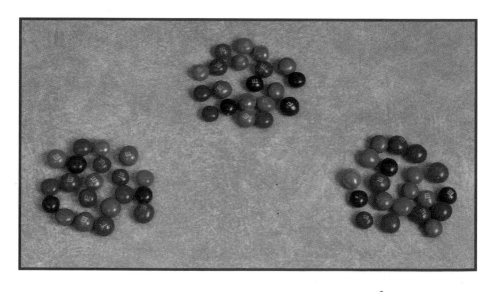

He eats **1** part.

To write a fraction showing how many parts he eats, put the number of parts he eats on top. ⟶ $\dfrac{1}{3}$

Put the total number of parts on the bottom. ⟶

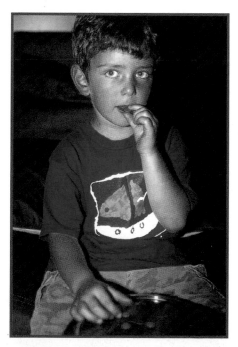

He eats $\dfrac{1}{3}$ of the candy.

This is **1** whole orange.

It is cut into **4** equal parts.

She eats **1** part.

To write a fraction showing the number of parts she eats, put the number of parts she eats on top. ⟶ $\dfrac{1}{4}$

Put the total number of parts on the bottom. ⟶

She eats $\dfrac{1}{4}$ of the orange.

When you share equal parts
with friends, each friend
eats a fraction.

This is **1** whole banana.

The banana is divided into **2** equal parts.

Each part is $\frac{1}{2}$.

Two friends each eat $\frac{1}{2}$ of a banana.

Here is **1** whole plate of cookies.
The plate of cookies is divided

into **3** equal
parts.

Each part is $\frac{1}{3}$.

Three friends each eat $\frac{1}{3}$ of the cookies.

This is **1** whole pizza.

It is divided into **4** equal parts.

Each part is $\frac{1}{4}$.

Four friends each eat $\frac{1}{4}$ of a pizza.

We may think we can eat
1 whole cake, but we can only
eat a fraction.

It is fun to eat fractions of cake
with our friends.

Words to Know/Index

Word Count: 375
Early-Intervention Level: 12